Bless YOUR Heart

Our Transplant Miracle

BRIGETTE MARIE WALKER

iUniverse®

BLESS YOUR HEART
OUR TRANSPLANT MIRACLE

iUniverse books may be ordered through booksellers or by contacting:

iUniverse
1663 Liberty Drive
Bloomington, IN 47403
www.iuniverse.com
1-800-Authors (1-800-288-4677)

Because of the dynamic nature of the Internet, any web addresses or links contained in this book may have changed since publication and may no longer be valid. The views expressed in this work are solely those of the author and do not necessarily reflect the views of the publisher, and the publisher hereby disclaims any responsibility for them.

Any people depicted in stock imagery provided by Getty Images are models, and such images are being used for illustrative purposes only.
Certain stock imagery © Getty Images.

ISBN: 978-1-5320-5528-7 (sc)
ISBN: 978-1-5320-5529-4 (hc)
ISBN: 978-1-5320-5542-3 (e)

Library of Congress Control Number: 2018909792

Print information available on the last page.

iUniverse rev. date: 08/21/2018

CONTENTS

DEDICATION

I would like to dedicate this book to my journalism teacher, John H. Gratton. He was the kind of teacher who made a difference in my life and gave me the courage to achieve my goals. In this teacher's eyes if you worked hard everything is obtainable.

ACKNOWLEDGEMENT

Our family will be forever grateful to the donor family. They gave my husband the gift of life and the opportunity to see our five sons grow up to be amazing young men just like their "Dad."

The Early Years

My decision to write our story and share our personal thoughts and experiences was a difficult decision. I believe everyone on earth has a destiny. I think sharing our story is fulfilling our destiny. Our life began ordinary and has turned out to be extraordinary. Hope you enjoy our story and will walk away never forgetting us.

Our love story began 23 years ago in 1995. I would have to admit my life really began at that time. After experiencing a miserable divorce, I had finally met a man who I knew was someone truly special and amazing. This man would be my "future husband." The man I want to share my life with forever. Dalton was introduced to me by my son's babysitter.

Coincidentally, Dalton had also recently been through a tough time, as he had gone through a divorce shortly before mine. This immediately gave us something in common. We had a connection. I think we both realized this connection from day one.

Dalton had 4 little boys. Their ages were 2, 4, 6 and 8. My son, Kyle was 4 at the time Dalton and I met. I knew Dalton was a good man. He loved his sons and anyone could see his love. My son also thought the world of Dalton. Dalton always treated my son, Kyle like one of his boys. His boys always treated me with respect and love. We felt like a family.

As I was going through my divorce I needed a place for my son and I to live. I moved into a house across the street from my baby-sitter. This was convenient and unbeknown to me was close to Dalton. He lived a few houses up the street. Was it fate or something greater?

In the beginning Dalton and I became good friends. My son and I would be playing in the front yard and Dalton would stop by to see how we were doing. I was blown away how nice this guy came across. I thought to myself he was too good to be true. I felt I was only seeing his good side. Was he a good guy? I realize I had trust issues. How do you ever get past this? I wanted to believe he was as wonderful as he seemed.

The First Date

A couple months went by and Kyle and I were settling into our routine life. I happened to be by myself on this particular evening, as I had to share my son with my ex-husband every other weekend. I believe Dalton must have known I was alone. I heard a knock at the front door. I went to the door and Dalton stood there. I could sense he was nervous. I invited him inside. After a few minutes of small talk, he apparently had gathered enough courage. He asked if I would go out with him on a date Fri. night. I said, "Yes". As I looked over and focused in on Dalton. He had a great big smile on his face. He later shared with me he was scared to death I would say no. I never really understood why he thought I would turn him down.

Having to share my son with my ex-husband every other weekend was hard on me. I felt very alone. I was looking forward to my first date with Dalton. I know you always hear people say this, but I felt like I had known Dalton all my life. Dalton was so easy to talk to and I felt comfortable and safe when I was with him.

This feeling gave me a sense of security when I was with him from the beginning. Fri. night finally came and Dalton arrived to pick me up. He planned a date night at the river boat casino. Before we left my house I inquired if he had made reservations. I knew we needed reservations or we would not be able to enter the casino. He looked at me with a deer in the headlights stare. He did not realize reservations were necessary.

He immediately tried to call but no reservation time was available. I told him not to worry we would be able to board. Upon arrival I told the customer service representative we had made reservations but I lost my confirmation number. Believe it or not we were able to board. I think Dalton was impressed with my negotiating skills. Thank goodness the night was saved!

We enjoyed a nice dinner and conversation. I recall thinking how I felt like I had known Dalton forever and this evening did not feel like a first date. I guess since Dalton's Mom had watched my son since he was 5 weeks old and I knew his mother. She was a good person and I was certain her son had to be a great man. Dalton's parents treated my son, Kyle like their own grandson. I would come by after work to pick up my son and they would have a new outfit on Kyle or a new toy to send home. I was lucky to have found such a great environment to leave my son as I never once worried about his care.

Now back to our first date. I wanted to know what Dalton did for a living and he said, "If I tell you I will have to kill you?" I immediately started laughing. He went on to say he worked for the government. I thought maybe he had a top secret position. Did he work for the FBI? Dalton also shared he had a side business he worked part-time doing foundation repair.

He was a busy man and realized he had to work hard to support his four sons.

I knew the date went well because Dalton had asked me out on another date before he even dropped me off from the first date. We always laugh at this, but I told him later I think I had to jump out of his car before it stopped when he dropped me off after our first date. Dalton did not walk me to the door, which struck me as being strange. We just said good-bye in his car and Dalton set up a time for the next date. Dalton explained later he did not want to put pressure on me to give him a kiss, so he did not walk me to the door. He knew I had been through a bad divorce and just wanted to give me some time and no pressure. I would guess this gives you some insight to his amazing personality. Never thinking about himself.

I asked him later why he always made sure he asked me out for a second date before the first one had ended. His answer was he wanted to be sure I did not have an opportunity to date anyone else. Pretty selfish don't you think?

On one occasion Dalton invited me to an outdoor Country Music Concert. I had not been to many concerts and love Country music so I jumped at the invitation. I had looked forward all week to the concert in anticipation. We arrived at the venue, parked the truck and began to walk with lawn chairs in hand to the concert.

We arrived at the gate with our tickets in hand and were advised we would not be able to take the lawn chairs in to the venue. Being the gentleman he was, Dalton said, "You go ahead and find us a seat and I will take the chairs back to the truck." I did not argue as we were parked a long way from the entrance. I proceeded into the venue and found a seat in the lawn. About 30 minutes passed and I kept looking for Dalton but he was no where in sight.

By this time the theatre was beginning to become crowded. I was starting to worry and then just realized I had Dalton's concert ticket in my pocket. I was not sure what to do. I was starting to have a panic attack. Was he still at the entrance trying to get inside? Finally, about 45 minutes later I see Dalton. We were both laughing as Dalton explained to the employee at the gate his story about taking the chairs back to his truck and letting his girlfriend go inside to find us a seat. Apparently Dalton must have been fairly convincing as they let him in the gates without a ticket. True story…. we can't make this up!!

Meeting The Sons

Our next date was probably more interesting as we took all 5 small boys out for pizza. I will never forget this night. Dalton was running around the table cutting up all the boy's pizza, pouring each child's drinks. He was like Super Dad! I only had to take care of one child and here Dalton was taking care of 4 small boys. You could tell he was more worried about the boys well-being more than he was about himself. I realized that night what a great Dad he was. Needless to say his nurturing and caring nature toward his sons impressed me more than anything he could have done.

I also loved how well the boys all got along with each other. They always seemed like real brothers. My son never felt left out and that made me happy. To this day my son thinks of all the boys as his brothers. When I hear him talk about any of his brothers he never calls them my step brother he always introduces each one as my brother.

Life As We Know It

4

Dalton and I continued to date and Dalton did always make sure he had a next date scheduled as apparently he did not want me to make a date with someone else. Dalton would always include our boys in our activities. I liked his approach as my son and his sons were important to us. We loved feeling like a family unit.

We began to travel to the lake a lot. Dalton's parents had a place at the lake in Grove, Oklahoma. Dalton grew up going to the lake house as a child. Dalton carried on this tradition with his family. The boys loved the lake. Everyone found the lake so relaxing. We had a swimming pool across from the house and the boys spent most of their time swimming. We would grill out and make Dalton's famous "Milkyway ice cream." If you have never had this ice cream, you are definitely missing out. All of our sons would jump on the golf cart and around the resort they would all go. Each one with a smile on their face.

Dalton bought a wave runner. He would give the boys rides close to the dock. I recall one time in particular Dalton took his youngest son, Tyler who was about 4 years old for a wave runner ride. He was on front of the wave runner when they started to do a donut. The wave runner tipped over. The whole incident seemed like it was in slow motion. Both Tyler and Dalton fell off into the lake. My heart went in my mouth. I was sitting on the dock watching the other boys swim. A few minutes later which felt like an hour later Tyler's small head came bobbling to the top of the water and Tyler was giggling so hard he ended up with hiccups. I was worried Tyler was hurt but he was having the time of his life. We had some good friends, Todd and Denise who also had a son who was about the boys age. His name was Steve. On occasion they would come down to enjoy the lake for the weekend. One particular weekend we all rented a pontoon boat and went out on the lake. We tied the wave runner on back of the pontoon and away we went. All the boys were having a wonderful time! We hit some rough patches on the lake and the pontoon began to take on water. We immediately headed back to the dock, praying the pontoon would not sink to the bottom of the lake. We had created another memory.

We made some amazing memories at the lake. We would play bingo at the deck by the lake. On occasion we would go into the small town to the Moose Club to play pool, dance and sing karaoke. I do recall one night when our friends, Todd and Denise accompanied us to the Moose Club. Denise and I decided we would sing a duet of karaoke. I have to admit we may have consumed a few drinks of liquid courage which was a Flaming Dr. Pepper to prepare us for our first stage experience. By the way if you have never drank a Flaming Dr. Pepper I would suggest everyone over the age of 21 should sample at least one!!

If my memory serves me correctly Denise and I chose a Beach Boys song classic of Fun, Fun, Fun – until Daddy takes the T-bird away! We belted out the song as Dalton and Todd sat in disbelief. I thought we sounded pretty darn good and apparently a few other regulars at the club must have enjoyed our singing as they asked my brother-in-law who happened to be a Moose regular when the "KC girls" were coming back to the Moose Club to sing! I guess Denise and I can relish in our 10 minutes of fame on stage in Grove, OK.

I recall another occasion the adults went to the Moose Club. This evening was a Toga party! My brother-in-law, Rodney pulled the sheets off his bed, tied some flashing head band on his head, and away we go. He was definitely partying it up that evening. Rocking Rodney as he had been nick-named was definitely the life of the party!! Everyone at the Club was commenting about his flashing head band. When we left that evening to return to the Lake house we passed through a sobriety check point. Rodney being consumed with liquor and thankfully not driving advises Dalton to pull over he knew these police officers. Oh my goodness!

Dalton takes one look at Rodney wrapped in a sheet and blinking head band and says, "Be quiet brother!" If we were pulled over just taking one look at Rodney we would all be thrown in jail without a doubt. Thankfully when we arrived at the checkpoint someone up above was watching over us, as the police had just received an emergency call and we passed through the check point quickly.

I honestly can admit life with Dalton there has never been a dull moment. He always plans many spontaneous events. One morning while I was at work Dalton called me to see if I had plans for Tues. evening. I said, "I was free." My son would be with his Dad. Dalton advised he had a surprise planned and to be sure to bring my swimsuit. We drove about one hour to Vinita Springs to a resort which was historical. The resort had relaxing outside hot tubs and beautiful waterfalls. We literally had to sneak inside. Ironically, we had spent the night at this resort as a paying customer a couple months prior to this visit. I had shared with Dalton how much I enjoyed that weekend at the resort. On this occasion we could not spend the night as we both had to work the next day.

Dalton came up with the idea to sneak in and we could relax and enjoy the hot tubs for an hour or so and then head back home. They had locker rooms so we both went in and changed into our swim suits and placed our street clothes in the locker. We relaxed in the hot tub and enjoyed the evening immensely. We even lost track of time and before we knew it was 10PM. We decided to go back to the locker room and change from our swim suits into our street clothes.

We noticed as we rounded the corner the door to the locker rooms was locked and the lights were turned off. Apparently the locker room closed at 9PM. We both looked at each other in disbelief. How would we get back into the locker room to retrieve our clothes?

Dalton went to the front desk of the hotel and shared we left our clothes in the locker room. The lady at the front desk said, "No worries we can just deliver the clothes to our room and wanted to know our room number." Dalton thought fast and said we are going to grab a bite to eat and we are wet. We just need to get dressed. At this point my heart was beating out of my chest. The lady at the front desk proceeded to call a security guard to retrieve our clothes from the locker room. As the security guard was carrying the clothes out of the locker room my hot pink panties fell to the floor and the security guard reached down to pick them up off the floor. I was thinking to myself just kill me now! Now I am certain my face had turned 3 shades of red. What else could go wrong? If this security guard knew the whole story Dalton and I would more than likely be hauled off to jail.

We still laugh at how crazy and spontaneous we were that night. I have never in my entire life participated in such craziness.

The Proposal
And Wedding

Dalton and I had been dating for a couple of years. One evening fairly close to Christmas Dalton appears in my kitchen carrying a small box with a beautiful ring inside and gets on one knee and proceeds to ask me to marry him. I said "Yes." I have to admit I knew Dalton was an amazing man, but I also knew my first marriage ended with a great deal of hurt. I wanted to believe Dalton would never hurt me. Dalton and I dated for six more years and then finally we were married.

Dalton without any warning, became ill just before we were married. This was the first indication of his heart issues. He went to the ER complaining of a terrible cough and was misdiagnosed with bronchitis. The Emergency Room physician reviewed his chest X-ray and discovered Dalton had enlarged heart. The doctor did not seem concerned about his condition but suggested Dalton set up an appointment with his regular medical doctor and the ER doctor released him to go home. Dalton was not feeling better after a few days so decided to make an appointment to see his personal physician.

Dalton calls me when he was leaving the doctor's appointment and asks if I could meet him at the hospital. Dalton was always being a jokester so I laughed and said, "Yeah right." Then Dalton's voice changed and he said "Really my doctor says I need to go the the ER." I dropped everything and immediately went to the hospital. Dalton was admitted into the hospital that evening. He was diagnosed with cardiomyopathy – congestive heart failure. Dalton's heart was enlarged to the size of a football. They pumped a ton of fluid from the heart. I was in disbelief. Dalton was very ill. I was in shock as Dalton had never been sick a day in his life.

The next morning Dalton's mom, Cindy and I were with Dalton at the hospital when the cardiologist came in his hospital room to see Dalton. I am still shocked by the news this cardiologist gave us. He said "Most people in Dalton's health condition only live a year." I think Cindy and I both looked at each other not believing this news. HOW could a perfectly healthy, never been sick a day in his life only have a year to live? I did not appreciate the doctor for saying this craziness in front of Dalton. Would Dalton just give up? The doctor planned to try to treat him with a new heart strengthening medicine but still did not give us hope.

I went home by myself and had a melt down. I hid from my son as I did not want to worry him as I knew Kyle was too young to comprehend this news. Heck I did not understand myself. I was sobbing like a baby on the couch. How could the dear Lord give me such a great man and then take him from me so soon? I was in disbelief but vowed at that point I would do everything in my power to save Dalton. I was not giving him up without a fight. I was sure he was not going to die on my watch!

Dalton and I were married in Eureka Springs, AR on Sept, 8, 2001. The small church was so beautiful overlooking a lake with gorgeous stain-glass windows. We had a tropical wedding! All the boys wore matching Hawaiian shirts like their Dad with colorful leis. My son, Kyle walked me down the aisle. Though a small wedding we were lucky enough to have all the people we loved with us sharing our special day.

The service was unforgettable. As we were about to say our "I do's" we heard a big clap of thunder and the rain came pouring down. Dalton had lost his father to cancer a few years prior, and we really believe his Dad was letting us know he was with us and giving his blessing on our special day.

Dalton and I honeymooned in Gulf shores, AL. Our timing was not the best as 911 occurred a couple of days prior to us flying to New Orleans. We arrived at the airport to an eerie sight. Bomb sniffing dog were being taken on the plane. We were all being patted down at security check points like criminals.

Traveling would never be the same. At one point I looked at Dalton and said, "Are you sure you want to fly?" In my mind I could visualize the plane flying into the Twin Towers only a a few days prior to our departure. My husband and I along with one other passenger boarded the plane. I admit my stomach did sink when I realized all the other passengers had cancelled their flight due to fear. Only 3 passengers on this flight to New Orleans. I believe we saw something we will probably never see again. Upon landing in New Orleans the flight attendants gave each other a hug, as if to say we are thankful we arrived and landed safely.

The story did not end there. We went to pick up our rental car. We noticed the lines were long and another couple saw our airline tags on our luggage. They asked if we just flew in and we said yes. This couple was trying to get home to Phoenix, AZ and had been stuck in the New Orleans airport for a couple of days. The flights had been cancelled due to 911 and now they were going to try to rent a car to drive home to Phoenix. Dalton and I could not help but feel guilty as we believe we might have been the first flight arriving New Orleans after 911.

We drove from New Orleans and made it to Gulf Shores, Alabama! We enjoyed our time which included walking on the beach. We had the good fortune to meet an interesting lady from Terre Haute, Indiana. She had driven to Gulf Shores to participate in a National Sand Castle Building Competition. She shared she was a grandma and loved to build sand art on the beach. Unfortunately, due to 911 the competition had to be cancelled though this was not stopping her as she had designed the most adorable dog in the sand I have ever seen.

As life happens we were heading back to catch a plane to return home from our honeymoon. We drove from Gulf Shores back to New Orleans. We stopped in the small quaint town of Foley, AL at a Mom and Pop café for breakfast. As you might know an older man comes in the café and inquires if we know the owner of a small red car. Dalton and I both look at each other and realized he was talking about our rental car.

This older gentleman who was on oxygen and I guess by mistake hit the gas pedal instead of the brake. Thankfully he had only damaged the bumper of our rental car and the car was still driveable. I felt sorry for this gentleman as you could sense this incident had definitely shaken him up. I hated to do it, but we called the police to do a police report of the accident. I knew we needed this report since this was a rental car and we did not want to be charged for the damage.

The New House /
Bittersweet Memories

6

We had not been married very long and realized with five sons my 1200 square foot house seemed way too small to accommodate our family. We kept the boys every other weekend and for eight weeks in the summer. We began looking and low and behold we found our dream house. Dalton and I found a gorgeous house house on 1 acre. I fell in love with the house. The great room had windows from floor to ceiling. The master bedroom had a fireplace and enormous whirlpool bathtub. We had plenty of room for the family. We made the big purchase and moved in.

Ironically our good friends Todd and Denise were moving into their new house the week after our move. So they helped with our move and we returned the favor.

Just before closing on our new house Dalton had a doctor's appointment with a new cardiologist Dalton's Uncle had suggested Dalton to schedule an appointment. Dalton called me at work and I will never forget this call. I could sense Dalton was upset, though he always put on a brave face for me. He went on to say he liked this lady cardiologist but she thinks I need a heart transplant. I was in shock and disbelief. Was this true? Never in a million years could this happen? After our conversation I literally had to get up and leave my desk as tears were streaming down my face. I felt so guilty for not going with Dalton to this appointment as I know he too was fighting off tears. Who wouldn't? This was so scary!

Dalton scheduled another appointment with this cardiologist to discuss going on a transplant list. I accompanied Dalton as he was not going through this ordeal alone. I loved him so much I wanted to be the person to give him strength and support. He needed a support system. I was determined I would be that person for him. Though I have to admit this would be a harder task than I could ever imagine. I kept thinking we just bought a new house. Can we afford it if Dalton is having health issues?

I loved Dalton's cardiologist. She was so caring about both of us. I am so thankful she was the person to be going through this journey with us.

She knew we were scared so she asked an 18-year-old young man to come in the office to talk to us. This young man sure did not look like he had a heart transplant. He was about to begin college and was athletic as he played on the basketball team. I know this gave Dalton encouragement. Dalton thought if he had a heart transplant he would not be able to work and would be confined to the couch "watching Oprah". He envisioned not being able to work and would basically be an invalid the remainder of his life. This young man made such an impression on both Dalton and I. I can still see this young man's face beaming as he described his active life after his heart transplant.

Dalton decided to go on the waiting list for a new heart. Honestly looking back, we did not have any other choice. Dalton's heart function was only about 20 - 25%. Dalton was placed in the hospital for an over night stay to be sure he was a candidate for a transplant. He was checked out from head to toe to be sure no other health issues or mental issues would be in the way to keep him from being added to the waiting list for a new heart. Dalton mentioned a psychologist came in to discuss how strong his marriage was.

Dalton advised the counselor his marriage was strong and we would be just fine through this whole journey. Hearing this news from Dalton made me so proud not only because I knew we had an amazing marriage but Dalton also realized this as well. I never had any doubt we would be together for the long haul.

Waiting For The New Heart:

After we decided to be placed on the heart transplant list in August of 2005. Dalton was given a pager and advised if the pager went off we would need to be to the hospital in 1 hour to prepare for surgery.

I always worried especially around the holidays if friends were at our house and if we received a page we would need to leave ASAP and head to the hospital. Dalton laughed and said you know I think they would certainly understand. Sounds pretty silly huh?

During our wait for Dalton's new heart my Dad was placed in the hospital about 1 ½ hours from home. My Dad was on dialysis and had a number of health issues. I was so torn on what to do. I did not want to leave Dalton just in case he received a page and we needed to travel to the hospital. Dalton being the wonderful man he was said, "You have to go see your Dad. He needs you." I went to see my Dad in the hospital and worried the entire time I was away. Would I make it back in time if Dalton's pager went off? Thankfully this did not happen!

We received invitations to go to several heart transplant support group meetings while waiting for Dalton's new heart. This allowed us to meet others who were like us on the waiting list or those lucky ones who had received a new heart.

On one occasion we took my son, Kyle to the transplant support meeting. I will never forget this meeting. A gentleman I would say in his early 50's shared his story. He had been seeing a cardiologist in another hospital. The doctor had basically told him he was terminal and there was nothing more they could do as his heart was failing. This doctor advised him he should plan to go home to get his affairs in order as he should be prepared as he was going to die.

Tears streamed down his face and also his wife was fighting back tears as he shared this story. I noticed Kyle, my son was also crying. This was hard for a twelve- year old to understand. Heck I did not even understand. Anyhow, this gentleman went on to share he was able to find another doctor in time. He was lucky and received a new heart. The heart transplant was a success and he was doing wonderful! We sure needed all the encouragement we could find.

We attended a transplant support meeting a few weeks later. One of the cardiologist shared a story of a King in a foreign country who traveled to the US to receive a transplant as his heart was failing. His Prince had traveled with him and wanted to give his heart to the King. Though the cardiologist went on to explain to the King and his prince this would not be possible. They would have to wait until someone donated a heart.

Dalton continued working but came home so exhausted every night. He would eat dinner and had to go right to bed as he was extremely tired. I knew his health condition was progressively getting worse.

I began to worry. What if he cannot make it until he gets a heart? I prayed a lot. I asked God to please help us endure until we received good news.

I was driving to work one morning listening to Paul Harvey discussing a study at a University up North in which was performed overseas, the study involved candidates whose heart function was similar to Dalton's and the heart was functioning about 20 – 30%. These individuals were given stem cell injections from their hip and injected into their heart. After this procedure, their heart function had improved almost back to normal. When I arrived at work I knew the same news cast would be on during lunch break. I ran out to my car at lunch to listen and wrote all the details down on paper. That evening I called and left a message for Dr. Richardson' secretary and explained of my husband's heart condition.

Unbelievably, Dr. Richardson called the house later this same evening and wanted to talk to Dalton. He advised Dalton a number of the candidates in the trial were in their 50's and 60's. He confirmed they had all shown improved heart function after the stem cell injection procedures. He explained the cells had basically rejuvenated the heart muscle. He went on to say he wished Dalton could have been in the trial as he did not have a candidate in their 40's. Dr. Richardson wanted to see the long term effects and if the heart function remained good over a period over time as you age.

The next day I contacted the heart transplant team to discuss our call with Dr. Richardson. I inquired if they had heard of stem cell used to rejuvenate the heart function. The head transplant coordinator, Kristina said she had not heard of this procedure and asked if Dalton wanted to be taken off the heart transplant waiting list. "That was not my intention." I told her. I went on to explain I was grasping at straws because I could see Dalton's health was failing and without a heart transplant I knew he would not be here. I was trying all options necessary to save his life. I was reaching out to anyone who could help. I guess until you are placed in this situation you could never understand. How do you watch the man you love slowly slip away? This was tearing me apart.

Much to our dismay, we found out later Kristina the heart transplant head coordinator discovered she had later stage breast cancer and decided to try a new drug in hopes of diminishing the cancer. I can not help but wonder if she ever thought of our phone conversation when I was trying to find a cure for my husband. Did she realize how precious life is? You can never know how you will handle a situation until you are thrown into one similar. I guess the old saying "Walk a mile in someone else's shoes."

The Page

In late Jan. of 2006 Dalton had a doctor's appointment. The transplant team determined Dalton would probably have to consider staying in the hospital until he received his heart. His condition was getting worse and he would have to be hooked up to machines at the hospital until he received a new heart. I was so worried.

Then a miracle…our miracle on Feb. 10th about 10:30 AM Dalton called me at work and advised he had received his page. He immediately contacted the transplant team as he had been instructed. The heart transplant team had advised him to make his way to the hospital. I ran in my boss's office to let him know Dalton received the call. I drove home in 15 minutes. Please realize my drive to work was normally 30 minutes. I think I cried all the way home and really don't recall the drive. I don't know if it was tears of happiness or if I was scared to death!

By the time I arrived home my Mother-In-Law was at our house prepared to ride to the hospital with us. Dalton seemed amazingly calm but this changed when he called my son at school as we were driving to the hospital. I looked in the rear view mirror and saw a tear run down his face. I think the realization of what was about to happen had settled in. Dalton had become such an amazing step dad to my son and they were so close. I thought I was going to start crying but I knew I had to be strong.

My brother-in-law drove to the hospital from Grove, Oklahoma to be with us during Dalton's six-hour operation.

Dalton, his Mom & I arrived at the hospital about noon. We were introduced to Connie. She would be our nurse to prepare Dalton for surgery. Connie hooked up all Dalton's IV's then she gave me some antibacterial soap and wanted me to scrub my husband's chest. I wonder if she did that so I would keep my mind off everything and focus on something else. I remember Dalton still seemed so calm. If I had been in his shoes I would have been having a panic attack.

The hardest moment was when all the boys came to see my husband before his surgery. I felt sorry for the boys as they seemed to be in shock not believing their Dad was going to receive a new heart. I know Dalton was so happy to see them. I know he had to wonder if this could have been the last time he would hug the boys.

At approximately 6PM Connie, our nurse was preparing to take Dalton for surgery. She also advised she would be leaving for the day as her shift was ending. I hugged her and told her I sure wish she could have stayed and appreciated all she had done for us to prepare my husband for surgery.

To my amazement Connie, our nurse came out to the waiting room to let us know at 7pm Dalton was doing well during the surgery. Bless her heart she had decided to stay and provide us updates on Dalton's surgery. I thought what an "angel" she was. Connie's children were 2 and 4 but she cared enough about our family to stay and let us know how Dalton was doing during surgery. Connie shared she had never seen a heart transplant. She gave us updates every hour.

I was nervous when Dalton went back to surgery but I had a feeling come over me I can only describe as a sense of peace. I had never had a feeling like this before. I felt like the dear Lord had wrapped his arms around me. I described this feeling I experienced later to a good friend and she said this feeling was our prayer circle of friends praying for Dalton while he was in surgery. Maybe she was right. We sure had some amazing friends who came to the hospital to sit with us during the six-hour surgery.

Dalton was the 277th heart transplant performed at this hospital. At midnight the surgeon walked into our waiting room to advise all of us Dalton's surgery went well. Dalton was in ICU for the night. He also mentioned "Don't be surprised if Dalton loves to shop". I love to go to craft shows shopping so this comment struck me as being funny. This was our only indication Dalton had received a women's heart.

In our miracle, I could not help but think of the family who lost their daughter. I was so thankful for their love. The hard decision the family made which saved my husband's life.

We discovered Dalton's heart came from a 26 year- old. We believe she was a police officer who had stopped a car for a traffic violation and while walking up to this car was shot by the driver. She was immediately taken to the hospital, and had been placed on life support for a month. I was so sad for her loved ones. She had not been married very long and was a step mom. My heart hurt for this family.

I know one day when we meet in heaven I can give her a big hug. What a blessing we received from her!

The Recovery

My mother-in-law and brother-in-law spent the night with me in the waiting room after Dalton's surgery. I went back every 30 minutes to peek through the window in ICU at my husband. He had so many tubes hooked up to him and honestly looked scary. Finally, the morning after surgery I could go in to his room to see him. I had to put on a gown and scrub down to prevent germs before I could enter Dalton's room. Dalton's immune system was weakened while on heart rejection medicine. I could not wait to kiss him. His color looked good but he seemed a little swollen. Even his hands were swollen. I helped him eat as it was hard to hold a fork with his hands being swollen.

In an effort to keep Dalton's spirits lifted our best friends, Todd & Denise decided we would all plan a vacation for all four of us later in the year when Dalton was feeling better. We thought this would give us all something to look forward to. We dreamed up a plan for a trip to Key West, Florida. We knew this would be adventure for all of us since we had never travelled to Key West. Nine months after Dalton's transplant, we planned to fly into Fort Lauderdale then rent a car and away to Key West.

A week prior to our departure Key West was hit with a major hurricane. We discovered the hotel we booked received so much damage they would be closed for a couple of months, for repairs so I went to work dreaming up plan B.

I found a cruise ship which traveled to Freeport, Bahamas then you could stay a few days at a beautiful hotel on the beach. I contacted the cruise ship to discover the ship had received damage during the hurricane. At this point we were all wondering if this trip was meant to be. I decided to check flights from Ft. Lauderdale to Freeport, Bahamas. If we could not get there by boat, then what about by plane?

I found a flight not realizing this was a 12 passenger plane. The day we arrived at Fort Lauderdale airport to catch a plane to Freeport we discovered at the airport check in counter, Dalton's birth certificate did not have a raised seal. The airline customer service agent hesitated to accept this for boarding then called his representative in the Bahamas and finally let him board.

While we were waiting to board, Denise would go over to stare out the window at the 12 passenger plane. About the third time I looked at her and shared with Denise the plane was not going to get any bigger by the time we depart and we would be just fine. I did not let her know but I was nervous flying on this small plane too. I had never flown on a plane this small ever before either.

To add to our fun, Todd's drivers license had expired 2 days prior to our trip and he did not realize. Every time we passed through security they would frisk him. We all laughed and at this point we named this the trip from Hell!!

Finally, we arrived at our beautiful hotel right on the the beach in Freeport. The entire hotel was surrounded with palm trees and gorgeous flowers with a tropical feel. The white sand and turquoise waters felt like a dream. I had never seen such a beautiful place. We had the most amazing vacation and fun time with our friends. This was a celebration for Dalton making it through his heart transplant. We all were beginning to think this trip was not meant to be, but ended up being the fondest memory. We all agree this was the best vacation we ever experienced.

Day by day while Dalton was in the hospital he began to get stronger. I was afraid to hug him as I was afraid to hurt his incisions in his chest. Matter of fact for the longest time I would not hug him. Dalton would have to hug me as I did not want to hurt him. I compared him to a china doll and I did not want to break him.

Dalton was in the hospital on Valentine's day so his brother, Rodney went to the gift shop to find me a card and some flowers on his brother's behalf since Dalton was not up to this task. They should have known Dalton's new heart was the best Valentine's present I could ever receive! Thank goodness I was going to have my husband back.

My son, Kyle came to the hospital to see Dalton. Dalton was doing so well I decided to go home for the night. My son and I stopped to get a hamburger. While waiting for food we both sat at the table and cried like little babies. I am sure if someone was watching us we looked like we were crazy.

We were so happy and relieved for Dalton. These were definitely tears of happiness. This ordeal had been a difficult and emotional six months for us all. We made it through this journey and Dalton was doing great. Our prayers were definitely answered.

Five days after surgery I brought my husband home from the hospital. I felt like I was bringing a new born baby home from the hospital. Upon arriving home, I cooked his favorite meals and whipped him up his favorite milk shakes. When he was in the shower I would warm up a towel in the dryer to wrap him up in. He was doing better everyday. We only had one issue. He was prescribed a number of anti-rejection drugs. We had to remember how much medicine to take each day. We literally had to take a class on how to administer his medications before we left the hospital. The drugs have to be administered correctly or you could die. The drugs keep your heart from rejecting a foreign object (the new heart). Matter of fact we heard a horror story of a heart transplant recipient who was trying to save money so cut his medicine in half. He died.

A good friend of Dalton's stopped by the house to check on Dalton after his surgery. I will never forget the words this friend said. "Man you are a miracle and I kind of like knowing a miracle." So true was his statement. Times in our life we need a reality check and Dalton received his. Sure makes you stop and realize you are just passing through on this earth.

My mother-in-law and I took turns the first week staying with Dalton during his recovery. I had to go back to work. Dalton was doing amazing but was not supposed to drive for 6 weeks due to his incision in his chest and if he was in an accident and the air bags inflated would possibly break open his incision in his chest.

Approximately 3 weeks after surgery I came home from work and strangely when I pulled in the garage I noticed a sack from Mc Donald's on a shelf. I also noticed the date from the receipt was that particular day. I took the sack in and inquired if Dalton knew whose sack this was? He started smiling and said it is mine. My husband went on to share his story. He said, "I was so hungry for a hamburger and decided I wanted to get out of the house today." I scolded him as if he was a little kid. "What would have happened if you were in an auto accident and broke open your chest." Dalton lowered his head in shame and I immediately felt bad. My goodness he had been through so much, I could not stay mad at him. If he needed to gain some independence and desired a hamburger, I guess by golly he had ever right.

Life After Heart Transplant

10

Amazingly Dalton has done wonderful after his heart transplant. He received an amazing heart. He works every day and owns a foundation repair business and employs two of our sons. This is a very physical and demanding job. Sure not sitting on the couch watching Oprah!

I often tease him the reason he was given a second chance was because he is so good with senior citizens. Dalton will provide a quote for a basement repair project for a senior citizen. Usually they have received a high quote from a big corporation and Dalton can perform the job for half the price.

He always says if this was my grandma I would sure hate for her to have to pay a high price for this work to be done. Dalton does not advertise for his business. His work speaks for itself as a neighbor tells another neighbor or friend of his hard work and reasonable prices. He receives so many referrals for a job well done. I am so proud of him and his hard work. This is not a 9 to 5 job. He works evenings and weekends. I am telling you he is the most dedicated person I know. Unless you share with someone nobody would ever know Dalton had a heart transplant.

If I could not love Dalton anymore than I do. He has always been there for me through the most difficult times in my life. When my Dad was in the hospital and an ice storm came my wonderful man loaded up his generator and away he went two hours away to save the day for my Mom. She was all alone and though she would have never admitted it, probably wondering if she would freeze to death by morning having no power and no heat. My sweet, amazing husband came to the rescue to save the day to set up his generator to be sure my Mom had power and would be warm. If that was not enough he stayed until her power came back on which took three days. He would drive my Mom to the hospital to see my Dad and then stop by for more gas to fire up the generator.

My Mom nick-named Dalton jokingly, "Mommy's little helper." After my Dad passed away and my Mom had surgery for a cancerous brain tumor. My Mother relied on Dalton to fix everything broken at her house. Dalton was her personal repairman. He repaired everything from a rattling gutter to a washer out of balance.

Sometimes I would apologize to Dalton for all he had to do for my Mom. He always said he never minded helping her. I truly believe it was the case. Dalton and my mother became close after spending hours visiting during the ice storm. My Mom enjoyed sharing her stories of her childhood with Dalton.

When both my parents passed away I could always lean on my Dalton. He has been such a strength to me. I realize how lucky I am to have met Dalton and so thankful he is in my life. I am so happy Dalton was given more time on this earth. He received an incredible heart. Dalton always says I was his Angel but that is not true. He is my angel on earth.

Scary Moments
At Work

11

About a year ago Dalton was by himself working to complete a job. He was in his enclosed skid steer loader when a middle-aged gentleman came walking up to Dalton. Dalton opened the glass door on his loader to see what this man needed. The man asked Dalton if he could have the lumber laying on the ground. Dalton advised he was just working at the site and the lumber was not his. Dalton told this gentleman he would need to discuss his request with the builder.

To my husband amazement, the man began to reach in his pocket to pull out a gun and asked Dalton to hand over his wallet. Dalton slammed his door on his skid-steer. He was thinking fast and in a split second shifted the skid steer loader into gear and headed toward the man holding a gun. He caught the man by surprise. The man holding the gun was knocked off his feet. I know this man was startled and surprised by this action.

With the man's legs pinned under the bucket Dalton proceeded to called 911 to report the crime.

Thankfully the police station was only 5 minutes away. A swarm of about 8 police cars surrounded Dalton's skid-steer loader. A policeman asked Dalton if he knew where the gun landed and Dalton replied he believe it maybe under the bucket. With guns drawn the police asked Dalton to slowly raise his bucket of the skid steer. Dalton did as he was asked by the officers and sure enough the gun was pinned under the bucket as Dalton thought. The police called an ambulance as they believed the man's legs may have been broken. Apparently it turns out the police discovered the gun had been stolen. This man had burglarized a nearby house the night before and also the gun had been stolen.

Dalton was driving home, understandably very shaken by all the events that transpired and planned to keep this a secret from me. He did not want me to worry unnecessarily. Though he began to think what if the police try to call the house. Dalton decided it would be wise to share this incident with me. He called me on his way home. I was so upset. I drove up to meet Dalton at his shop. I could not help but think if Dalton had not reacted fast, he could have been shot and I would be planning his funeral. This incident stirred up the same feelings I experienced when Dalton was waiting on his page to receive a new heart. I don't know what I would do without him. He was my soul mate and I sure did not want to live my life without him.

Giving Back

Dalton has given time to offer encouragement with individuals waiting for heart transplants. Dalton is the poster boy for heart transplants as he has been so lucky and never experienced heart rejection. He has been healthy. He has visited other patients waiting for hearts in the hospital. We realize how difficult it is to wait for a new heart. We have been down this same road.

We have had the good fortune to meet so many heart transplant recipients and their families. We went to the yearly heart transplant picnic a couple of years ago. I still think of this family to this very day. The man who was in his thirties had recently had a heart transplant. He was on regular rejection medicine and due to the cost he had been switched to take the generic version of the medicine. He was able to return to work but ever since the switch to generic medicine, he had been passing out at work.

Unfortunately, his health insurance would only pay for the generic version of the medicine. I suggested they contact the drug companies directly to see if they could offer assistance. How sad? Why are the drugs so expensive? If we did not have decent health insurance Dalton would be in the same predicament. I sometimes wish I could help all these good people who cannot afford the anti-rejection medicine. They are trying to work to keep their health insurance and still having a tough time affording the medicine.

A number of people who have heart transplants usually go on disability to help pay for the medicine. This was not an option for Dalton. I think working and having his own business has kept him healthy. He does not have time to be sick. Dalton leaves an incredible legacy to his sons. He has instilled in our sons to be hard working and treat people the way you want your grandparents to be treated.

Empty Nest

Our sons have all moved out of the house and have lives of their own. Making their way in the world. We feel so fortunate to have raised our sons together. We are a happy family.

Dalton continues to spoil me as he always has done. My big 50th birthday my wonderful husband scheduled a five-day cruise with all 5 of our sons and their significant others. Our youngest son, Tyler who is a Marine drove from North Carolina to be with us. He wanted to surprise me, so arrived a day early.

We all cruised from Tampa, Florida to Cozumel and Cayman Islands. Everyone had a great time. Definitely made memories which will last a lifetime. We drove jeeps in Cozumel and swam with the Stingrays in Cayman Islands.

We love to travel when we have an opportunity. We realize life is so short so we take advantage of our precious time together. We have been to beautiful white sands in the Bahamas, fed the Flamingos in Aruba on Flamingo Island, watched the waterfalls at Niagara Falls, taken a riverboat cruise at Lake Tahoe.

How lucky we have been! We definitely have a greater appreciation of life. I am so very grateful for every day I have with my Dalton! Bless Your Heart!

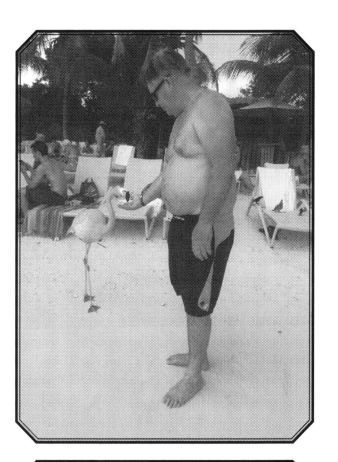

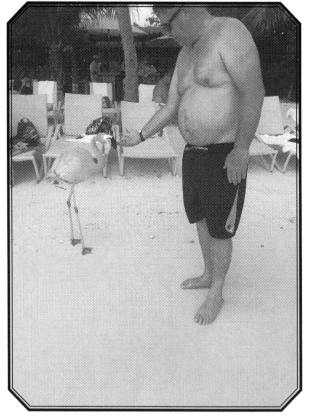

ABOUT THE AUTHOR

Brigette grew up in a small rural town in Missouri. Her father was a second generation sawmill operator. Her mother was a stay at home Mom and bookkeeper for her father's sawmill business.

Brigette, always was a "daddy's girl," and has fond memories of accompany her Dad to the sawmill. She would ride on the bulldozer sitting right beside her father, built bon-fires to roast hot dogs and marshmallows, played on the tire swing in the big oak tree, near the sawmill. She has so many happy memories during her childhood days.

Brigette excelled in Journalism class and enjoyed writing stories for the local newspaper. One day a week she would assist the editor laying out the newspaper before going to printing. She was always anxious to see the finished product.

Brigette graduated proudly as Salutatorian of her class. One week after her graduation she was hired for a position as a customer service representative. She enjoyed her career and worked for this particular company for twenty-two years.

Brigette loves to travel and would prefer to land anywhere with a beach and palm trees. In her spare time, she loves practicing her cake decorating skills for her family and close friends.

RECOGNITION
WITH ALL MY GRATITUDE

A good friend of mine said it best, "Surround yourself with people you love and truly care about you."

These special people deserve to be remembered and thanked as part of our journey.

Thank you to the cardiologist, surgeon and nurses. I appreciate the thoughtful nurse, who knew I did not want to leave my husband's side and I shared I thought I was parked illegally in the Emergency Room parking. This nurse replied, "Don't worry honey, if you receive a parking ticket I will take care of that ticket for you!"

Another special nurse cared enough about her patients to bring in her own combs and shampoo. In her own words, "The hospital only supplied no lather shampoo and cheap combs." Might seem like a small gesture to some but meant the world to us.

We are thankful to make new friends at the

transplant group meetings. Sharing their stories and comparing notes during and after our journey.

Thank you to my wonderful mother-in-law. I won the lottery when I received Cindy as my Mother-in-Law. She was always there for our family.

Thank you to my brother-in-law. Lucky to have you! "Uncle Rodney"

We appreciate all the laughs. We needed your humor.

Thank you to my best friend. You are a sister to me, Denise.

You have seen me through my highs and lows. You are the best! We are so happy Todd and Steve are part of our family too. Love you all. Thank you guys for sitting with us during Dalton's six- hour surgery. Keeping us all calm.

Thank you to our special Aunt and Uncle. You were so sweet to make us delicious meals when we came home from the hospital. We owe you so much!

We appreciate our work family. We have worked with some amazing friends. They stepped up to assist us in our time of need and offer us encouragement.

Lynette,

You realize God places special people in your life. You are definitely one of those special people. I looked forward to coming to work everyday because of you. Appreciate you keeping my spirits lifted.

Thank you to all our sons. You were meant to come into my life. What joys you have all brought to me.

Bless my Mom and Dad. Due to my Dad's health issues they could not be at the hospital but called every hour to check on us. You knew they wished they could be with us. Thank goodness you made me a strong person to come through this journey smiling.

Thank you to my hubby. You are the love of my life, my soul mate. The dear Lord blessed my life to be able to spend every day as your wife.

Thank you, dear Lord. You answered all our prayers. We know we would have never made it through this journey without all your love and blessings.